We All Matter

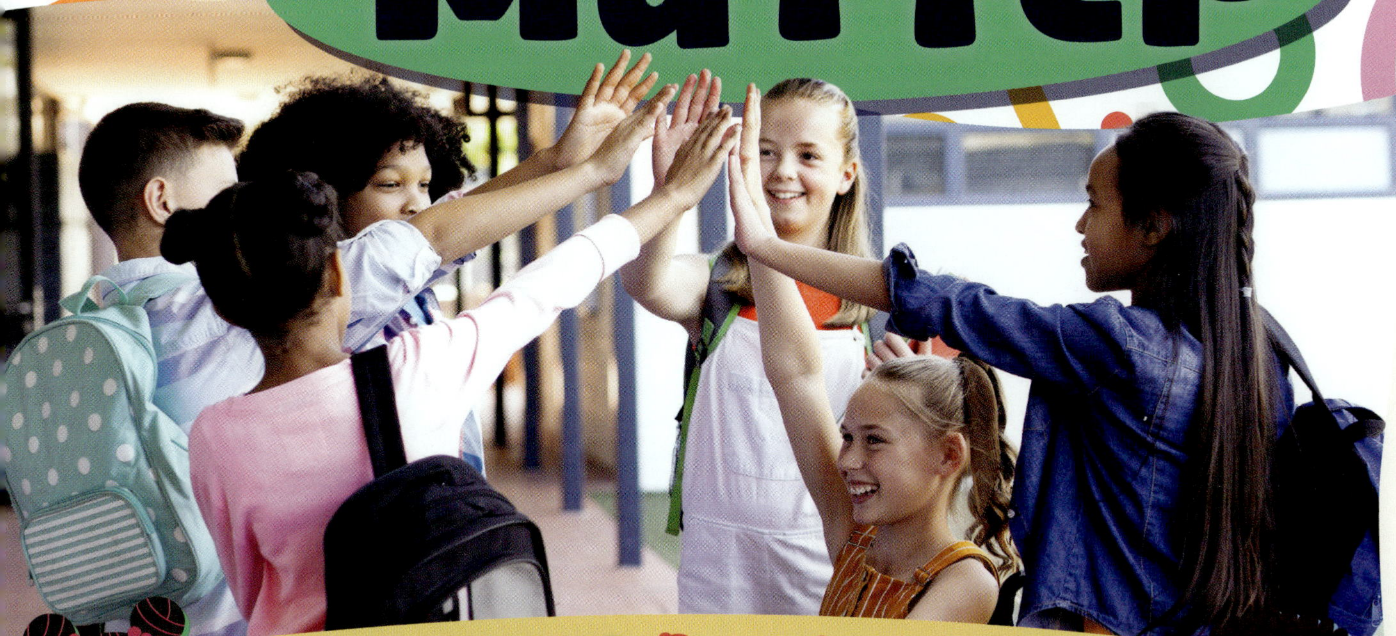

Guess What? People Matter!

Written by Charis Mather

Published in 2026 by
KidHaven Publishing, an Imprint of
Greenhaven Publishing, LLC
2544 Clinton St., Buffalo, NY 14224

Written by: Charis Mather
Edited by: Noah Leatherland
Designed by: Amelia Harris

Cataloging-in-Publication Data
Names: Mather, Charis.
Title: We all matter / Charis Mather.
Description: Bufalo, New York : Kidhaven Publishing, 2026. | Series: Guess What? People Matter | Includes glossary and index
Identifiers: ISBN 9781534550308 (pbk) | ISBN 9781534550315 (library bound) | ISBN 9781534550322 (ebook)
Subjects: LCSH: Bullying—Juvenile Literature | Interpersonal relations—Juvenile Literature | Perception –Juvenile Literature
Classification: LCC BJ1475 M38 2026 | DDC 177--dc25

Manufactured in the United States of America

CPSIA compliance information: Batch #CSKH26
For further information contact Greenhaven Publishing LLC at 1-844-317-7404.

Please visit our website, www.greenhavenpublishing.com.
For a free color catalog of all our high-quality books, call toll free 1-844-317-7404 or fax 1-844-317-7405.

Find us on

Image Credits

All images are courtesy of Shutterstock.com, unless otherwise stated. Cover – roshenshami, EZ-Stock Studio. Recurring – Dedraw Studio, Lubo Ivanko, toranosuke. 4–5 – Robert Kneschke, 2xSamara.com. 6–7 – NadyaEugene, JLco Julia Amaral, PeopleImages.com - Yuri A, hedgehog94. 8–9 – Andrii Zastrozhnov, Dean Drobot. 10–11 – Prostock-studio, Media_Photos. 12–13 – Pixel-Shot, PeopleImages.com - Yuri A. 14–15 – SynthEx, Impact Photography. 16–17 – Evgeny Atamanenko, SeventyFour. 18–19 – SeventyFour, WESTOCK PRODUCTIONS, CandyRetriever, ESB Professional, Ruslana Iurchenko, ChiccoDodiFC, Sabelskaya, JeremyShow. 20–21 – Drazen Zigic, New Africa, Teran Studios, Ljupco Smokovski. 22–23 – Africa Studio, Robert Kneschke.

Contents

Words that look like **this** can be found in the glossary on page 24.

Guess What?

Nobody is exactly the same. We are all different in our own ways. We all have our own lives and our own stories.

And guess what? We all matter!

Even though everyone lives their own individual lives, that does not mean that we live in separate bubbles. The things we do and the choices we make affect the people around us.

We All Matter!

Our society is made up of the people around us. Everyone in a society has a different part to play in the community. It can take time to find where we fit, but that is normal.

Some people make great leaders. Some people work best as part of a team. Some people are most comfortable helping out quietly by themselves. Wherever we fit in, we are all equally important.

Communication Is Key

Since so much of life involves other people, it is important to know how to communicate. Communication involves sharing your thoughts, feelings, and other information. It also means listening to what others have to say.

It is possible to communicate without spoken language.

Give people your complete attention when they are communicating. Your body language can help show others that you are listening. If something is not clear, you can ask questions to make sure you understand someone.

Standing Up and Standing Out

Everyone has rights, and they deserve to be treated fairly. This includes you! It is important to stand up for yourself if people ignore your rights or treat you unfairly.

Sometimes, standing up for yourself means saying "no" to people who do not respect your rights.

Ask a trusted adult about your rights. They can teach you how to stand up for your own and others' rights safely. They can show you what to do in a dangerous or uncomfortable situation.

Building Better Relationships

We build lots of different kinds of relationships during our lives. Relationships can be positive or negative.

In a negative relationship, someone might...

- Disrespect you
- Try to control you
- Make you feel bad
- Treat you unkindly or unfairly

In a positive relationship, someone will...

- Be honest
- Treat you kindly and fairly
- Show you respect and trust
- Not be controlling

When you make friends, think about how you can help build positive relationships.

Keeping Your Cool

You might not get along with everyone you meet, and you might disagree with people you do get along with. The best thing you can do is stay calm and respectfully communicate.

Sometimes, talking a problem out can help you see it from a different point of view. Then, you can work together to find a solution that you are both happy with.

Teamwork Works

One of the most important skills you can have is working well in a team. A good team is made up of people who are patient and willing to listen.

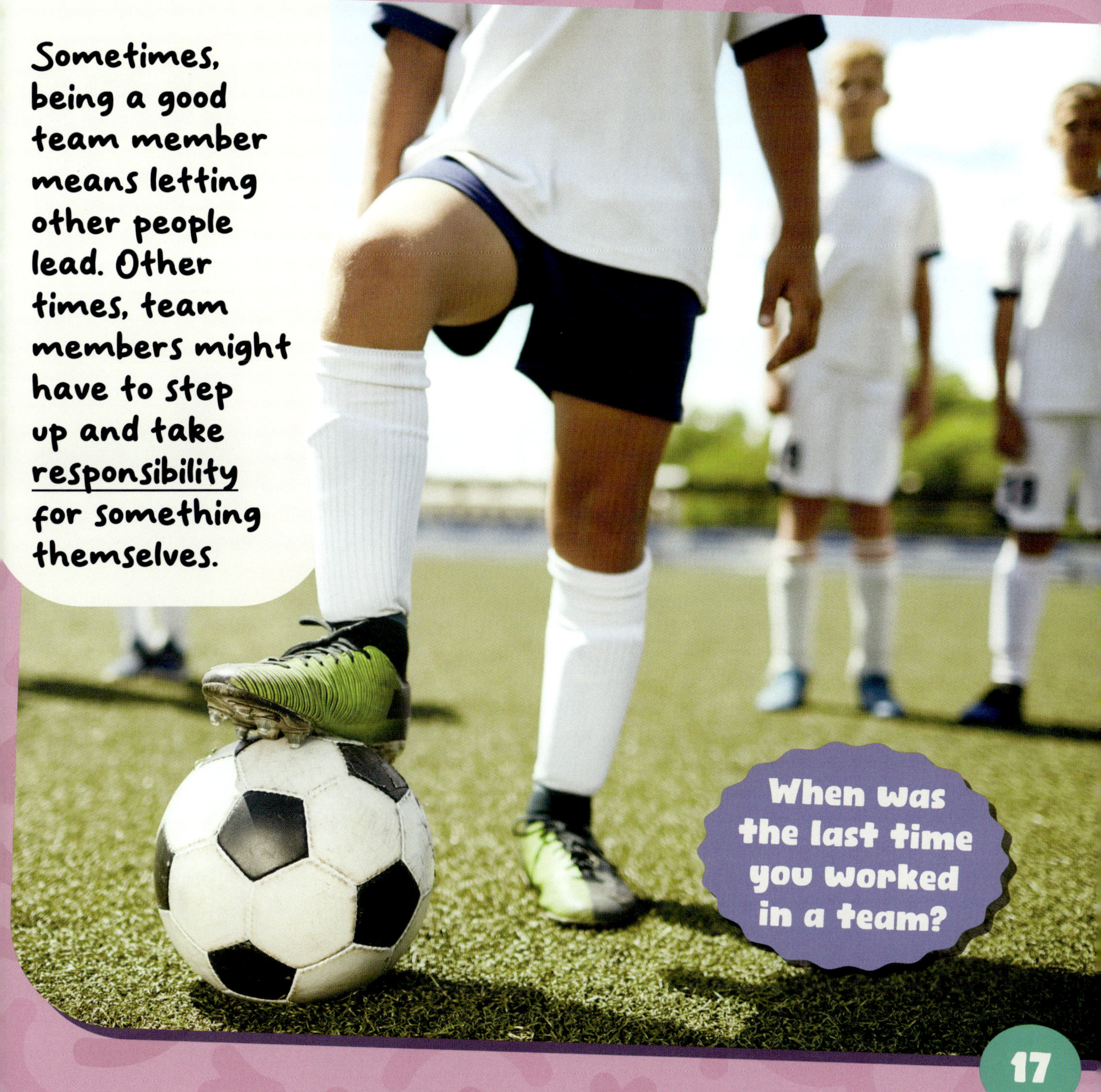

Sometimes, being a good team member means letting other people lead. Other times, team members might have to step up and take <u>responsibility</u> for something themselves.

When was the last time you worked in a team?

Lifelong Learning

Everyone has had their own experiences that shape the way they see the world. This means that there are always things that we can learn from others.

Different cultures might do things differently than what you are used to. Just because you do things a certain way does not necessarily mean your way is better than someone else's way.

Healthy Habits

As you learn more about the world and about yourself, you might want to make changes to the way you live. One of the best ways to make lasting changes is with healthy habits.

Habits are things that people do often.

In Your Home

Learn to solve disagreements by talking problems out.

In Your School

Talk to your teacher if you see a classmate being treated poorly.

In Your Community

Find out if you can help people in your community by volunteering.

People Matter!

Everyone in a society has a responsibility to look out for each other and treat each other well. There are so many different ways we can care for people in our communities.

How could you help in your community?

We are all human. That is why it matters that we have the right attitude toward each other. No matter how different we are, we all matter!

Glossary

body language	things a person does with their body that show how they feel
community	a group of people who are connected by something
cultures	the traditions, ideas, and ways of life of groups of people
disrespect	to treat someone in a negative or insulting way
respect	a thoughtful and polite attitude toward people, rather than a judgemental or rude attitude
responsibility	the things that people have to or should do
rights	freedoms and abilities that people have as humans, which should not be taken away from them
volunteering	helping others for free

Index